Hypnosis to treat Tremors

Mike Valmar C. H.

INDEX

TERMS OF USE AGREEMENT

The author and publisher have used their best efforts in preparing this book. The author and publisher make no representation or warranties with respect to the accuracy, applicability, fitness, or completeness of the contents of this book. The information contained in this report is strictly for educational purposes. Therefore, if you wish to apply ideas contained in this report, you are taking full responsibility for your actions.

EVERY EFFORT HAS BEEN MADE TO ACCURATELY REPRESENT THIS PRODUCT AND IT'S POTENTIAL. HOWEVER, THERE IS NO GUARANTEE THAT YOU WILL IMPROVE IN ANY WAY USING THE TECHNIQUES AND IDEAS IN THESE MATERIALS. EXAMPLES IN THESE MATERIALS ARE NOT TO BE INTERPRETED AS A PROMISE OR GUARANTEE OF ANYTHING. SELF-HELP AND IMPROVEMENT POTENTIAL IS ENTIRELY DEPENDENT ON THE PERSON USING OUR PRODUCT, IDEAS AND TECHNIQUES.

YOUR LEVEL OF IMPROVEMENT IN ATTAINING THE RESULTS CLAIMED IN OUR MATERIALS DEPENDS ON THE TIME YOU DEVOTE TO THE PROGRAM, IDEAS AND TECHNIQUES MENTIONED, KNOWLEDGE AND VARIOUS SKILLS. SINCE THESE FACTORS DIFFER ACCORDING TO INDIVIDUALS, WE CANNOT GUARANTEE YOUR SUCCESS OR IMPROVEMENT

LEVEL. NOR ARE WE RESPONSIBLE FOR ANY OF YOUR ACTIONS.

MANY FACTORS WILL BE IMPORTANT IN DETERMINING YOUR ACTUAL RESULTS AND NO GUARANTEES ARE MADE THAT YOU WILL ACHIEVE RESULTS SIMILAR TO OURS OR ANYBODY ELSE'S, IN FACT NO GUARANTEES ARE MADE THAT YOU WILL ACHIEVE ANY RESULTS FROM OUR IDEAS AND TECHNIQUES IN OUR MATERIAL.

Chapter 1

Can You Hypnotize Me to Believe in It?

The Webster's New International Dictionary defines hypnosis as "the induction of a state resembling sleep or somnambulism, which is called hypnosis or hypnotic sleep. Also loosely - the induced state of hypnosis."

There are degrees of hypnosis which have been characterized as "lethargic, cataleptic, and somnambulistic hypnosis; and again, simply as light and heavy hypnotic sleep, with corresponding variations in suggestibility

However, Encyclopedia Britannica further states "there remains no generally acceptable explanation for hypnosis, though one prominent theory focuses on the possibility of discrete dissociative states affecting portions of consciousness."

The word hypnosis is derived from the Greek word *hypnos*, meaning sleep. Hypnotism is often presumed to make someone go under a state of reduced consciousness while the person remains awake. The general behavior of those under hypnosis are being extremely positive to suggestions, and achieving a high level of relaxation. Daydreaming is another activity likened to hypnotism, wherein a person looks oblivious to his surroundings yet experiencing heightened imagination – depending on how light the trance is.

There are two ways by which hypnosis is performed: (1) hetero-hypnosis, wherein a hypnotist induces a state of being in trance and being open to suggestions; and (2) auto-hypnosis, wherein the state is self-induced.

The results are the same. Any suggestion that is carried out a period of time after hypnosis, is known as post-hypnotic suggestion.

Believe it or not, we experience being hypnotized everyday – following the definition of hypnosis as being in a trance-like state, or intensely focusing on a particular activity/subject thus tuning out almost everything else internally and otherwise.

Ever been so engrossed with a movie or a book that you did not immediately notice someone calling you already at the top of his voice? Reading, writing, closely listening to a record are examples of activities that can put us in a light trance, and altering our attention such that we can become extremely attentive to these, that we unconsciously shut off outside subjects vying for our attention.

Furthermore, we sometimes become so affected by the imaginary world of a daydream or a chapter of a book that our emotions take over. We cry over an affecting song, feel fear as the villain gets near the hero's hiding place, or even scream over a particularly frightening scene.

This kind of phenomenon, referred to as self-hypnosis, is so common and so human a trait that Milton Erickson, a hypnotism expert in the 20th century, concluded that people hypnotize themselves on a daily basis.

Note then, that this kind of "everyday trance" is different from the trance brought about by deep hypnosis, and is comparable to that relaxed mental state between wakefulness and sleep. There is also a difference between auto-hypnosis, where the state of extreme suggestibility is self-induced; and hetero-hypnosis, where it is induced by a hypnotist or another person. All these we will try to explain further in the succeeding chapters.

In all of the above mentioned categories, the hypnotized person, as stated in the Encyclopedia Britannica, "seems to respond in an uncritical, automatic fashion, ignoring aspects of the environment (e.g., sights, sounds) not pointed out by the hypnotist. Even the subject's memory and awareness of self may be altered by suggestions, and the effects of the suggestions may be extended (post-hypnotically) into the subject's subsequent waking activity..."

In self-induced hypnotism, a person feels relaxed and very open. As in while buried in a book or engrossed in a film, concerns about the "real world" seems forgotten for a while and temporarily escaped from.

This is parallel to hypnosis with the aid of a hypnotist. If the hypnotist states the person under his "spell" is in extreme heat, the person may start to sweat and experience high temperature, even if it the atmosphere is perfectly fine. If he suggests to a timid and painfully shy person that he is in fact an extremely confident man who is so sure of himself, the person may suddenly feel open to socializing with other people, strangers even.

But every person practicing hypnotism worth his work is the first to admit that the effect is only temporary. For example, a person can be made to quit smoking by suggesting through hypnosis that the smoke is poisonous and deadly. That person then starts to become adverse to smoke, and feel nauseous whenever he gets near it. Thus, he may

Hypnosis to treat Tremors

shun cigarettes. But if this is not followed up by corresponding therapy and other methods geared for long-term results, the habit will come back eventually.

Another proven limitation of hypnotism is even while under it, a person's common sense, principles, beliefs and life convictions remain unchanged throughout and after the experience. No one can also be hypnotized against his will, because the mind has to be willingly and consciously open to be affected by the hypnotist's suggestions.

For example, hypnotism cannot make a Muslim eat pork or a Superman fan fly out of a window. Since the mind is still fully alert – only this time the subconscious is more open – the person's sense of safety is still on guard. His sensibilities will continue to govern his decision-making process.

Then again, we can never really be sure. One story goes saying a man, undergoing hypnosis to boost his self-confidence, was told by the hypnotist that he "could do anything, anything as long as he puts his mind into it." For more effect, the hypnotist says: "Why, you could even rob a bank if you want to." Although the hypnotist may have meant the statement only as a metaphor, his subject then proceeds to rob a bank a couple of days later!

A study says that on the average, 25 out of 100 people can be hypnotized very easily. Almost all children belong to this group, who are perceived to be highly susceptible to suggestion. This ratio varies according to the hypnotist's personality, technique, and experience. The success of the hypnotist also depends on the subject's personality, attention span, and mental status at the moment. Interestingly, while it seems rational that persons with high intellect cannot be easily hypnotized because of their capacity to process all information that gets into their brain – it is in fact the opposite. It is believed that intelligent people are also the most creative – thus they can easily associate the hypnotist's word play with their own visual or sensory representations.

Chapter - 2 Tremors

Tremors are sinusoidal contractions in the limbs that are caused by contractions in the muscles. In layman terms, tremors refer to rhythmic jerking in muscles of the limbs. They are involuntary movements of a body part. This happens as a result of irregular contractions in the muscles of the limb. The affect is the opposite. For example, muscles that contract results in the bending of the wrist. Simultaneously, under the effect of other muscles, the wrist is extended. The result is a recurring movement of the wrist. This can happen in any part of the body, but is usually more common in hands, feet, and head. Moreover, these movements cannot be controlled. They are sometimes seen to be triggered by some factor such as age, alcohol, different neurological diseases and some medicines.

Tremors are symbolized by shaking of certain limbs, head, shaky voice, or difficulty to hold anything, and also trouble in writing or drawing.

Have you experienced sudden trembling in your limbs, or your head that could not either be explained or controlled? If so, how do you decide if this fact is worrisome or not?

Essentially, tremors are divided into two types: normal tremors and abnormal tremors. Tremors can either be caused by simple physiological reasons, neurological issues, physical problems, or psychological disease.

Normal tremors (physiological tremors) are the minor jerks we experience occasionally. These hardly interfere with our life nor are they detectable by a normal eye. The reasons behind these tremors are not yet identified. They are most definitely not connected to any serious disease though

Abnormal tremors, as the name suggest, have a more sinister reason behind them. Also referred to as enhanced physiological tremors; these tremors can be due to several psychological and pathological reasons. Drug abuse, withdrawal, or a medical drug reaction is another cause. Furthermore, unlike the normal ones, advanced physiological tremors are more than noticeable by others.

They also dreadfully interrupt the lifestyle of its bearers. Such is the intensity and recurrence of the tremors. This person can be rendered crippled till the shaking subsides. These tremors usually occur in the far limbs but their affect lingers onto the rest of the body including the head, tongue, vocal cords etc.

Tremors can be further classified as:

Type	Symptoms	Common Causes /Common groups
Rest Tremor	These tremors appear usually in the limbs of the body when they are in a relaxed position. Essentially, rest tremors occur in the limbs where the muscles are not contracted and are supported against gravity. For example, a hand hanging by the side or resting in the lap. These tremors disappear when the limb moves.	Parkinson's disease Wilson's disease Essential tremors (discussed later)
Postural tremors	These turmors happen when a limb is supported against the act of gravity. Thus a person may experience these tremors standing up, doing something or sitting down but not when he is	Essential Tremors Alchohol withdrawals Metabolic disorders Post-traumatic tremor

	lying down.	
Action/ Intention Tremors (Cerebellar tremor)	These tremors are experienced when a person is in the midst of doing an action or beginning to prepare for it. The action that cause the tremor usually requires precision and concentration such as aiming for the target. Naturally, the person will be forced to interrupt the action.	Stress and Anxiety Primary writing tremor
Action/ Task specific Tremor	Usually happens during a specific action. Such as hand tremors while driving a car, writing on chalboards etc	Stress and Anxiety Primary Writing Tremor Vocal Tremor

Tremors as a disease

When tremors become constant enough to disrupt the normal routine of a person, a health check is due. For as you probably know by now, tremors do not necessarily have harmless reasons behind them. They can mean something much more threatening. The tremor types which can be accounted under tremors as a disease are discussed below. These tremors are classified and diagnosed with respect to their origin, duration and frequency

Essential Tremors:

The Movement Disorder Society's Tremor Investigation Group defines essential tremor as a bilateral, largely symmetric postural or kinetic tremor. These tremors involve hands and forearms that is visible and persistent. Also, there is no other explanation for this. These tremors are a form of abnormal tremors, that pose as mild tremors at first. Initially, they are usually seen to effect one side of a person's body. They are gradually dominant over the other side as well (appearing usually after the age of 40). Although the frequency decreases as the patient grows older, the severity increases. Thus rendering the person crippled at times. This may stop them from doing their normal duties. Essential tremors, are said to be triggered by stress, anxiety, exhaustion, or low blood glucose levels. Patients have a 50% chance of passing it on to their next generation. The causes of essential tremors are yet unknown. It also seems that the cerebellum as well as some other neurological components are affected. Hand tremors are the most common symptoms of essential tremors. These tremors are noticeable in certain actions or postures (postural tremors as well as intention tremors). The essential head tremors, another feature of essential tremors, cause the head to nod or shake repeatedly. According to a report by the World Health

Organization, ten million people in the US alone suffer from Essential Tremors.

Parkinson Tremor

Just as essential tremors manifest themselves in tremors in half the body, Parkinson tremor also affect half the body. Although later engulf the rest of the body as well. Moreover, Parkinson tremors are also triggered and inflamed by stress or anxiety. But unlike essential tremors Parkinson is the resting tremor (discussed in the previous section). It is seen to be one of the first symptoms of Parkinson's disease as well. The cause of which are degeneration of the structures in the brain that monitor movement. Parkinson tremor is referred to as the 'pill-rolling' tremor. This person usually has the motion of the thumb and the fingers as identical to the motion of a pill being rotated.

Other tremor types include:

- Dystonic tremor (this is among people with dystonia)
- Psychogenic tremor (also known as hysterical tremor, this tremor is known for its sudden onset and remission and unpredictable changes in direction)
- Rubral tremor (slow tremors of rest, posture and intention type)

Disorders and other causes of tremors

1. Familial inheritance
2. Neurodegenerative diseases such as Parkinson's
3. Drug abuse or withdrawal
4. Multiple sclerosis

5. Stroke
6. Brain injuries and resulting trauma
7. Fear (which usually cause hand tremors)

Immediate causes of tremors
1. Low glucose level in blood
2. Stress and anxiety
3. Deficiency of some nutrients in body
4. Strong emotions
5. Exhaustion of body

How are the patients affected?
According to Differentiation and Diagnosis of Tremors by Crawford P and Zimmerman EE, here are the findings. Enhanced physiological tremors can work to seriously disrupt the lives of the patients in many ways. According to various surveys, the most common forms of tremors are head, hand, and vocal tremors. These three tremors can render the patient unable to perform simple everyday tasks.

Consider this: a patient suffers from hand tremors as a result of essential tremors. These hand tremors are of the task-specific type. Thus, they are specifically triggered when they are planning to write something down. This incapacitates them from writing. This can be a serious drawback in their personality which may disturb them psychologically.

Not only is the patient in danger of hurting themselves physically, but they can sink into further depression. According to several doctors, tremors follow a cyclic order in many cases. Anxiety may cause tremors, but the prospect of tremors itself lead to further anxiety!

The tremor sufferers are unjustifiably introduced to shyness and embarrassment. They become more reclusive with time and refuse to socialize. If the case worsens, they may refuse to go out into public at all.

Hypnosis

Hypnosis: A Brief Background

To truly understand the term hypnosis, let us look deeper into the meaning of this word.

History itself proves that hypnosis is a time honored therapy. Civilizations all over the passage of time have used hypnosis. They have designed this to remedy their problems, with specific chants, songs, and rituals. They believed that mind and body are inter-connected. They also believe that the well-being of one can produce the well-being of others.

Hypnosis, as a process, was initially studied from a 'magical' and rather 'magnetic' point of view. This was stated by its initiator Anton Mesmer. He believed that human beings had a fluid, a magical potion like quality to them. He also thought this could produce the act of healing. He successfully cured many diseases by passing magnets over the bodies of patients. To his surprise, he soon discovered that he could heal without the magnets. He had unintentionally stumbled upon one of the most coveted healing powers of the modern era!

Hypnosis was initially introduced by James Braid in 1841 as *hypnos*, the Greek word for sleep. Later, it was renamed to neuro-hypnosis which was shortened to hypnosis. This is translated to *nervous* sleep, or the sleep of the senses.

James Braid, along with his friend Dr. James Esdaile, worked side by side, experimenting with this newfound power. They employed the fixed-gaze method. Later, the Esdaile state to prepare patients for surgeries. This was performed on them with mind-boggling success and was virtually painlessly, even through their surgery.

Several researchers, hypnotists, and psychiatrists thus began to use this method. Once it was officially approved for therapeutic methods, it was used widely, producing incredible results.

Hypnosis: as a definition

According to the American Psychological Association Division 30, the process of hypnosis typically involves an "introduction to the procedure. During which, the subject is told that suggestions for imaginative experiences will be presented. The hypnotic induction is an extended initial suggestion for using one's imagination. It may contain further elaborations of the introduction. A hypnotic procedure is used to encourage and evaluate responses to suggestions. When using hypnosis, one person (the subject) is guided by another (the hypnotist) to respond to suggestions. Changes in subjective experience, alterations in perception, sensation, emotion, thought or behavior" can then be made.

Hypnosis: as a process

In lay terms, hypnosis is preceded by its induction. Afterwards, continuing on to whatever transpires in the hypnotic state of the patient. Usually the hypnotic suggestions, and concluding with the termination of the hypnosis. The testing of the hypnotic suggestions may also be included in the process.

The goal of a hypnotist is to mellow a mind to do an action, or accept a suggestion which it consciously would not.

Essentially, hypnosis requires two people, the hypnotist, and the subject. Hypnosis may also be induced by one own self which is known as self-hypnotism.

Hypnotic induction:

In this process, the subject is to be pulled deeper into his subconscious state, that is the alpha mind.

The setting for this phase is very crucial. Where some hypnotists play soothing music, some especially emphasize upon the overall 'feel' of the place. That is, they insist that the room needs to be pleasant, inconspicuous, noise proof and completely relaxing.

Exercises are set for the subject that would relax the subject's body, lulling them to a relaxed state. There are several procedures for induction, such as music therapy, showing pictures, fixed gaze induction and many more.

The subject is instructed repeatedly by the hypnotist to relax himself, and to perform certain exercises. They also include induced imagery instructions. This is where the subject is asked to cast different imageries to trigger his subconscious mind. In my sessions, I also use the eye lock, and feeling more relaxed from head to toe method. This is excellent for those clients that have problems "seeing" something pictured in their minds.. I back this up with the "counting method" to help deepen the trance. This way, they do not have anything to imagine in their minds. Everyone knows how it feels to relax, but they may not be able to "picture" a white fluffy cloud to relax.

The subconscious state:

The suggestions are given to the subject in a clear voice. Essentially, the ailment of the subject is tackled here. It is important for the hypnotist to know the nature of ailment of the subject. He employs different techniques in this phase to command the subconscious of the subject. This will help to ensure his cure.

The waking state

The subject is requested to (via imagery or simple instructions) wake up. The counting procedure is helpful here. The beta mind starts to take over and it is preferred for this process to be slow. You do not want to shock the person into abrupt wakefulness.

Hypnosis to treat Tremors

Hypnosis: As a method

Practically, hypnotizing includes 4 tasks:

1. Induce trance
2. Deepen that state
3. Suggestions and commands
4. Reversal from the trance.

- Before starting with the induction, it is preferable to inform the patient about the procedure. You would also inform them about the benefits in an encouraging manner. Phrases like, "hypnosis is a great cure and totally natural" or "It leaves you relaxed, with your inner fears gone." You may also state that so many people have gone through it. Explain that they are in for a wonder soothing experience." banish qualms from the minds of the subjects. Gain their confidence, and make sure they understand it is not black magic, or witchcraft.
- Next follows the selection stage. This is where the hypnotist performs certain tests to ensure the subject's ability to follow commands, and take suggestions.
- Induction is, as described above. The hypnotist usually suggests the subject to get

in a relaxed posture, before continuing on to further conditioning.

- Deepening is the continuation of conditioning, where the subject is drawn deeper into compliance.
- Healing phase is a crucial one. Suggestions, motivations, cleansing, confessions all are a part of this phase. Mike Valmar, a certified hypnotist, uses *regression* to treat tremors caused by stress or anxiety. Regression involves taking the subject back to the time before the traumatic incident. We then lead the client slowly to the incident. We then make their subconscious understand it. We then delete the trauma issue from the mind that resulted in tremors.
- Bringing back from trance, or "waking up" is done slowly, and carefully. We do not want to shock the subject. We want them to know where they are, or what has been suggested to them. All the while, the client is instructed that they are happier, more relaxed and re-vitalized. And they really are, that's the magic of it all.

Hypnosis: what does it do?

1. Anti-aging
2. Health propelling
3. Disease cures
4. Compulsive behavior cures

5. Polishes interpersonal skills
6. Aid pregnancy and childbirth
7. Treats addictions
8. Establishes emotional stability
9. Banishes depression
10. Helps deal with grief and loss
11. Teaches calming techniques
12. Aids relationship building
13. Polishes parenting/job/interpersonal/personal skills
14. Treats phobias
15. Induces fitness and healthy living

Hypnosis: misconceptions

As stated in the section of history, hypnosis was a method that was distrusted. The reason for this is that initially, it was associated to magic. The power to force people do something which they, in their consciousness, would abstain to. Moreover, in the Middle Ages, when the Church was at its zenith, pain was considered to be a bad fate. It was believed that the bearers had to suffer, so avoiding it was considered unthinkable. Although this theory is obsolete today, it was the basis of the initial hesitation towards hypnosis.

In these recent times, people are still skeptic of the hypnotic cure. They fear that they will be conditioned to do something immoral. Or something they would not be aware of otherwise. The main questions people ask regarding hypnosis, shows their concern. It clearly reflects what the society collectively thinks. Some people regard it as magic. Some believe that people can be conditioned to do anything, even against their own will. They believe the hypnotist can take over their mind and body. It is also believed, we can do this without them being aware of it. These are simply the wrong messages propagated by our media. Hypnosis is simply the safest and the most natural cure, for most complex problems. Professional hypnotists are trained personnel who have attended classes on the subject, and may bear authorized permits and/or licenses. Certification and laws differ from state to state. If you seek a hypnotist, the main thing is to confirm their training. Ask if they have worked with your issue or bad habit before. It's time the society realizes this amazing therapy, it's benefits, and what can be done through hypnosis.

Mike Valmar: A Case Study

The issue of having tremors is very important to me, so I wanted to include my own experiences with you here. My skill as a hypnotist has established me as a local hero for my work in helping others. My comedy hypnosis shows have brought fun and excitement to others as well. As a person who suffered with tremors, I know the important roll hypnosis provides in the control of tremors.
Hypnosis has changed my life, and it can do the same for you.

I was a talented DJ back in 1980s, leading a perfectly content life. I had found my calling as a DJ, and was earning a wonderful living and doing what I always wanted to do. Little did I know that my life would soon change in the next two years to come.

In 1982, I encountered a brutal accident that totaled my car. Miraculously, I survived almost unscathed. I later learned that the wounds went much deeper. I later noticed my hands shaking in a weird manner. This was to the extent that I could not hold a newspaper or a cup, without shaking. I was now being embarrassed by even the most simple tasks. I then decided to visit several doctors and was referred to specialists. I had to pay colossal bills to somehow stop the tremors. People kept asking me "What's wrong with you" or

"Are you ok" But the one that hurt the most is when they thought I was on drugs, or having withdraws. I know something had to be done. None of the medicines or the treatment could completely cure me. I thought I was doomed with these awful tremors. I had to pay attention to everything I did. I thought my hands would tremble forever. This would disable from holding anything and thus causing a spectacle. I could not hold a newspaper and read it. I had to place it flat on the table. I could not carry two things at one time. I could not do any work with my left hand, and would not even think of drinking hot coffee with it.

Hypnosis was introduced to me in passing and to my amazement, I seen definite progress. After only one session, I had the complete use of both my hands. No more exorbitant bills to my doctor, no more monthly medicine bills.

Completely taken in by this miraculous therapy, I jumped at the chance to be certified as a hypnotist. One of my friends told me I had a charismatic personality. That furthermore, I had a definite stage presence, ideal for a hypnotist. Intrigued, I began to research on this field and was soon taking courses to learn more. I attended classes throughout the state, and became a hypnotist. I practiced, learned from the best, and gained the experience I needed. I run my practice as a leading hypnotist of my field. But I did not stop there. Even now, I'm taking various courses to extend my learning, and thoroughly enjoying my service to humanity. I'm always looking for ways to improve myself, and my practice. I keep up on my CEU's (college education units) and always strive to be the best in everything I do. Currently, I own and manage a DJ service in Florida, a comedy show (with it's theme as hypnosis) and the hypnosis therapy service. The hypnosis business (Advanced Hypnosis Centers). Hypnosis is an incredible thing. It is safe, relaxing, and has hundreds of uses. It has worked for me, and thousands of others. I know it can work for you.

Thank you,

Mike Valmar

http://www.AdvancedHypnosisCenters.com

Printed in Great Britain
by Amazon.co.uk, Ltd.,
Marston Gate.